Alex Ovechkin

By Jeff Savage

AMAZING ATHLETES

Lerner Publications Company • Minneapolis

Lerner Publications Company
A division of Lerner Publishing Group, Inc.
241 First Avenue North
Minneapolis, MN 55401 U.S.A.

Website address: www.lernerbooks.com

Library of Congress Cataloging-in-Publication Data

Savage, Jeff, 1961–
     Alex Ovechkin / by Jeff Savage.
       p. cm. — (Amazing athletes)
     Includes bibliographical references and index.
     ISBN 978–0–7613–7672–9 (lib. bdg. : alk. paper)
     1. Ovechkin, Alexander, 1985–—Juvenile literature. 2. Hockey players—Russia (Federation)—
Biography—Juvenile literature. 3. Hockey players—United States—Biography—Juvenile literature.
4. Washington Capitals (Hockey team)—Juvenile literature. I. Title.
     GV848.5.O94S38 2012
     796.962092—dc22 [B]   2011004825

Manufactured in the United States of America
1 – BP – 7/15/11

TABLE OF CONTENTS

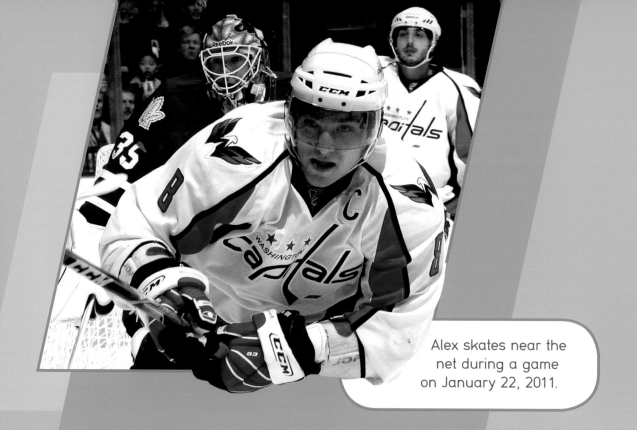

Alex skates near the net during a game on January 22, 2011.

FROM LAMB TO LION

Washington Capitals player Alex Ovechkin waited near the net. He looked for the puck. His face was scary. He was missing a tooth and had a crooked nose. A **defender** tried to push Alex away from the net. Alex sent the defender to the ice.

Alex and the Capitals were playing this 2011 game against the Toronto Maple Leafs. Nearly 20,000 fans had packed the Air Canada Centre in Toronto. Millions more watched on TV. They saw Alex near the net, waiting to pounce.

Alex was ready. The puck came toward him. He tipped it with his hockey stick. The puck sneaked into the net for a goal. "You have to fight for that puck," Alex said afterward.

Alex reaches out to tip the puck for the first goal against the Maple Leafs.

Alex was born in Russia. His last name means "little lamb" in Russian. Alex acts like a lamb with children. Before the game, he met with a boy whose father had been killed a year earlier. Alex gave the boy a signed photo and a jersey. But when the game starts, Alex turns from a lamb into a lion. He plows through opponents. He races to the puck. He shoots with brute force.

Alex battles for the puck.

In the third **period**, the Capitals hung on to a 1–0 lead. Alex was near the net again. Teammate Mike Green sent a shot toward the goal. A defender blocked it. Alex swooped in. He flicked a **wrist shot** between the **goalie's** legs for the score! Alex and his teammates celebrated.

Alex celebrates with teammates after his third-period goal.

The Leafs scored to cut the lead to 2–1. The Caps answered to make it 3–1. In the final moments, the Leafs removed their goalie. In his place was an extra **attacker**. Capitals player Nicklas Backstrom sent the puck along the left side of the ice. Alex blew past defender Tomas Kaberle. Alex controlled the puck on the end of his stick. He flashed toward the goal and fired a shot into the back of the net!

Fans tossed their hats onto the ice. Three goals by one player in a single game is called a hat trick. People throw their hats out of respect. The Capitals won the game, 4–1. "I had three lucky goals," Alex said. "I'll take the win."

Moscow is the capital of Russia.

RUSSIAN DYNAMO

Alexander Mikhaylovich Ovechkin was born September 17, 1985, in Moscow, Russia. He weighed more than 12 pounds at birth. His mother, Tatyana, was a basketball star. She won gold medals at the Olympic Games in 1976 and 1980. Mikhail, his father, played professional soccer. Alex had two older brothers, Sergei and Mikhael.

Alex and his parents watch a hockey game in 2004.

The Soviet Union was a group of states, which included Russia. Moscow was the capital of the Soviet Union. When Alex was born, the Soviet Union was in trouble. Its **economy** was in ruins. Alex's family lived on the edge of the city in a rough neighborhood.

Alex was two years old when he first held

a hockey stick in a store. He was five when he saw his first game on TV. Alex cried for his father to let him watch the game. But Alex did not start playing hockey until he was eight. His brother Sergei encouraged him.

Alex competed against older boys. He learned quickly. At the age of 10, he once took a shot that hit the goalpost so hard that the puck broke in half. Alex practiced outside on a frozen pond. Friends would join him for a while and then leave. Alex would stay for as long as eight hours at a time. He had sandwiches and a thermos filled with tea from his mother.

When Alex was a child, he was a big fan of Pittsburgh Penguins player Mario Lemieux. Lemieux and the Penguins won the **Stanley Cup**, hockey's championship trophy, in 1991 and 1992. Alex collected Lemieux's hockey cards.

"We couldn't get him off the ice," said his father. "We weren't forcing him. Hockey was his passion." Alex's parents encouraged him to do exercises to build strength. The family lived in a top-floor apartment of a 10-story brick building. Alex did not ride up the elevator. He ran up the stairs.

In 1995 Alex's brother Sergei was killed in a car accident. The tragedy crushed Alex. To help him deal with the loss, he devoted himself completely to hockey. Over the next few years, he grew strong and learned a lot about the game.

In 2001, at age 16, Alex left his school team to join Dynamo Moscow, one of the top Russian hockey teams. "You dive into sport with your head and arms and legs, and there's no time for anything else," Alex remembers. "There's

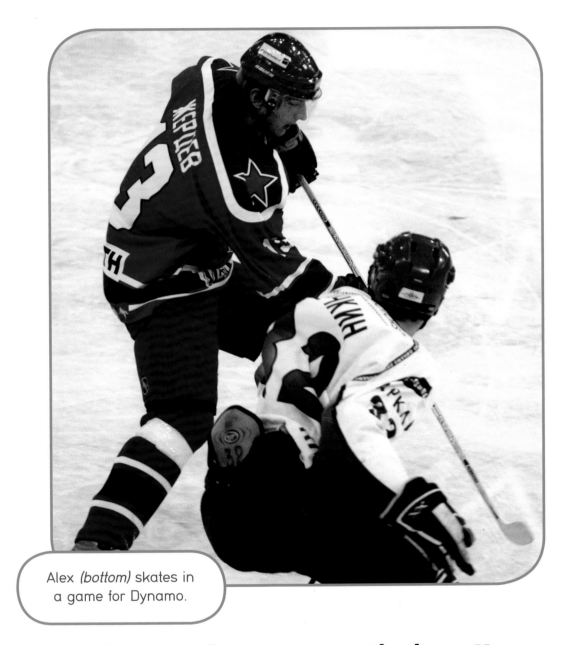

Alex *(bottom)* skates in a game for Dynamo.

no other career." Dynamo gave Alex hope. He wanted a better future for himself and his family.

Alex shoots the puck through the legs of Team USA player Ryan Suter during the World Junior Championship.

"TONS OF FUN"

Alex was a blur on skates. He was a magician with the puck. Through exercise, his legs became as thick as tree trunks. "Without training, I am nothing," he said.

Soon after joining Dynamo, Alex led the Russian Junior National Team to a gold medal at the World Junior Championship. He had hat tricks against Switzerland and the United States. The next year, he became the youngest member of Russia's national team.

Alex was a fan of the National Hockey League (NHL). The NHL is the top hockey league in the world. At the age of 19, Alex was eligible for the 2004 NHL **draft**. The Washington Capitals held the first pick. Their choice was easy. They selected the Russian star.

Alex smiles after being selected as the first pick in the 2004 NHL draft.

Unfortunately, the NHL's owners and players were arguing about money. The 2004–2005 NHL season was canceled. Alex stayed in Russia to play one more season with Dynamo.

In summer 2005, the owners and players ended their argument. The 2005–2006 season was on. The Capitals offered Alex a three-year **contract** worth $12 million. Alex was rich!

Alex bought a house near Washington, D.C., where the Capitals play. He lived there with his parents and brother Mikhael. His mother cooked and did laundry for the family. His father gave Alex simple advice: "Be yourself, be respectful, and that's it."

Alex is like a rock star, but he tries to stay humble. The owner of one Washington, D.C., nightclub says, "He's more down to earth than any of the other athletes in Washington."

Alex's first pro game was against the Columbus Blue Jackets. He scored two goals! Opponents were dazzled by Alex. "He has tons of fun playing," said Ottawa Senators goalie Ray Emery. Coaches were impressed too. "He's 230 pounds of pure muscle, speed, and competitiveness," said Nashville Predators coach Barry Trotz. Alex was named to the NHL **All-Star** Team. He also won the Rookie of the Year award.

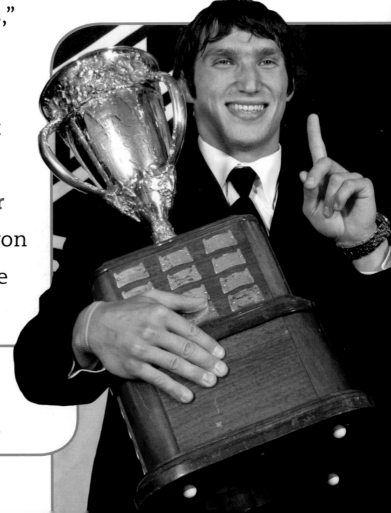

Alex holds the Calder Memorial Trophy. It is awarded to the NHL Rookie of the Year.

Alex scores the game-winning goal for Russia in a 2006 Winter Olympics game against Canada.

KEY TO THE CITY

Alex proudly played for Russia at the 2006 Olympic Games. He scored the game-winning goal to beat Canada. But the Russians failed to win a medal. In the 2006–2007 NHL season, Alex scored 46 goals to lead the Capitals. But the team finished last in their **division**. Alex was not used to losing.

Alex raised his game. By the 2007–2008 season, he was unstoppable. Goalies were helpless against Alex. He seemed to score at will. Opposing coaches **checked** (guarded) him with two or three players at a time. This created more room for Alex's teammates. The Caps started winning.

Two New Jersey Devils players check Alex during a 2008 game.

Alex was in the final year of his contract. Caps **general manager** George McPhee wanted to keep Alex. He and team owner Ted Leonsis met with Alex to discuss a new contract. They agreed on a 13-year contract for $124 million. It was the richest deal in NHL history! "Alex is a once-in-a-generation player and an even better person," Leonsis said after the deal. "We are lucky and proud to have him here in Washington, D.C."

Alex likes to visit Russia in the summertime. A Russian magazine called him the country's most eligible bachelor. "Moscow is a big city," Alex says. "It's all nerves—something's always happening somewhere. D.C. is a quiet, calm family town. If you compare Russia and America, they are two different worlds."

At a 2008 game in Montreal, Canada, three weeks later, Alex suffered a broken nose. But he stayed in the game. Alex scored three goals to force **overtime**. Then he won the game with his fourth goal. "Today was a special day," he said. "I broke my nose. Have stitches. Score four goals."

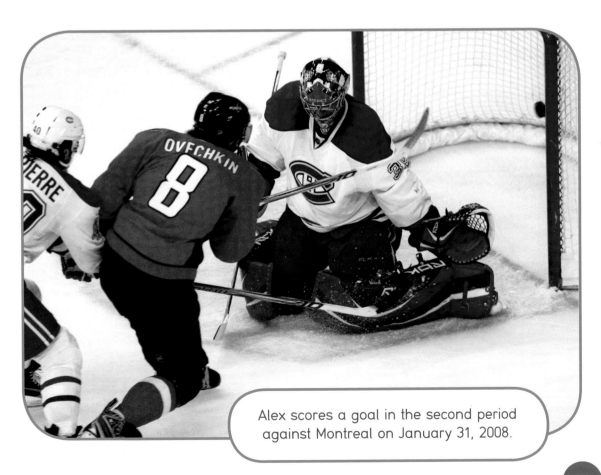

Alex scores a goal in the second period against Montreal on January 31, 2008.

Late in the 2007–2008 season, Alex scored his 60th goal. He was the first player in 12 years to reach 60 goals in a season. He finished with 65. As a result, the Caps had the best record in their division. They faced the Philadelphia Flyers in the first round of the playoffs. The Caps pushed the Flyers to seven games before losing the series. The season was a huge step forward for Alex and the Capitals. Alex won the Hart Memorial Trophy as the league's most valuable player (MVP).

Alex *(center)* waits near the net for a pass during a game against the Flyers in the 2008 playoffs.

Alex holds up his key to the city of Washington, D.C., in 2008.

A ceremony in downtown Washington, D.C., was held in Alex's honor. Mayor Adrian M. Fenty gave Alex a key to the city. This was a big honor for Alex. The huge crowd cheered. "Today is a big day. I have a key for the city," Alex announced through his gap-toothed smile. "And I am the president this day in the city, so everybody have fun—and no speed limit."

Capitals fans wearing Alex Ovechkin
jerseys cheer at a 2010 game.

OVIE

Alex was wildly popular now. His jersey was
the league's best seller. Everyone called him
Ovie. "At restaurants, they don't care if we
come in, just as long as he shows up," said
teammate Mike Green. "Everybody wants to
meet Ovechkin. They want to see him and be
around him."

The Capitals won their division again in 2008–2009. Alex led the league in goals again. Capitals coach Bruce Boudreau said: "We'd be nowhere without Alex."

This time, the Caps won their first round playoff series by beating the New York Rangers. "He's amazing," Rangers center Chris Drury said of Alex. "There aren't enough words in English or Russian to describe him."

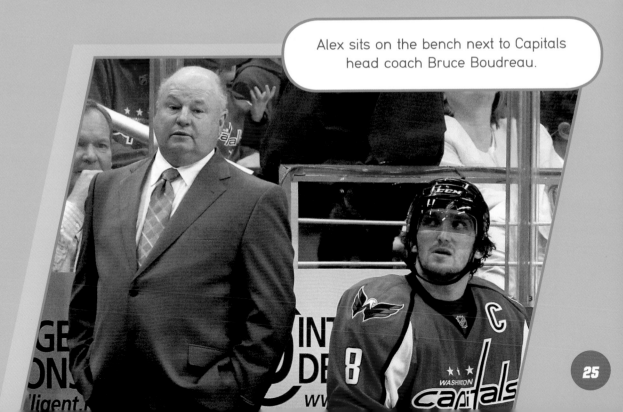

Alex sits on the bench next to Capitals head coach Bruce Boudreau.

In the second round, the Caps faced the defending Stanley Cup champions, the Pittsburgh Penguins. In Game 2, Alex scored a hat trick. The Caps won the game, 4–3. The series was close, but the Penguins won in the end. After the season, Alex was named league MVP again. It had been more than 10 years since a player had won the Hart Memorial Trophy two straight years.

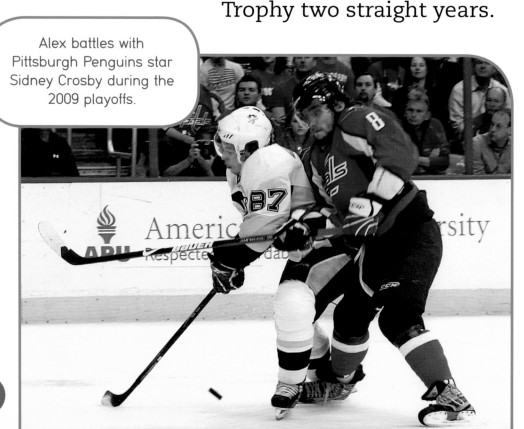

Alex battles with Pittsburgh Penguins star Sidney Crosby during the 2009 playoffs.

Alex takes to the ice for the first time as the captain of the Washington Capitals.

Ovie fever was at an all-time high. Every game in Washington for 2009–2010 was sold out. In January 2010, Alex was named team captain. The letter C was sewn onto his jersey.

Alex led the Caps to the best record in hockey in 2009–2010. He was voted the league's MVP for the third straight year. But Montreal knocked the Capitals out of the playoffs. "We know we can win [in the playoffs]," Alex said, "but we don't. It's hard."

Alex will continue to win awards. But he says he would "trade them all for one Stanley Cup." To help reach that goal, Alex will keep training to get faster and stronger. He will come to practice early. He will keep a positive attitude. Above all, he will focus on what matters most. "I want to be the best. Just the best," Alex says. "I want to win the Stanley Cup. I must work. I must learn."

Alex likes to make time to sign autographs for young fans. "They are fans of our team. They want my signature. If you have time, why not sign them all?"

Alex signs an autograph for a fan before a game.

Selected Career Highlights

2010   Won the Hart Memorial Trophy as the NHL's MVP for the third time
Named First-Team All-Star for the fifth time
First player ever to be named First-Team All-Star in first five
   seasons of his career
Led Capitals to the division title and the Presidents' Cup (best record)
Played for the Russian National Team at the Olympic Games

2009   Won the Hart Memorial Trophy as the NHL's MVP for the second time
Named First-Team All-Star for the fourth time
Attempted most shots on goal in a season by a left winger in NHL
   history (528)
Led Capitals to division title

2008   Won the Hart Memorial Trophy as the NHL's MVP for the first time
Named First-Team All-Star for the third time
Scored the most goals in a season by a left winger in NHL history
Set Capitals team record for goals in a season
Led Capitals to the division title
Led Russia to a gold medal in the World Championships

2007   Named First-Team All-Star for the second time
Led Capitals with 46 goals and 96 points

2006   Won the Calder Memorial Trophy as the NHL's Rookie of the Year
Led all rookies with 52 goals and 54 assists for 106 points
Named First-Team All-Star for the first time
Scored the most points in a season by a rookie left winger in NHL
   history
Played for the Russian National Team at the Olympic Games

2005   Joined the Washington Capitals
Scored two goals in his first NHL game

2004   First overall selection of the NHL draft
Named to the Russian National Team
Youngest player (age 19) to compete in the World Cup of
   Hockey

2003   Named the team captain of Russian Junior National Team

2002   Led Russia to a silver medal in the World Under-18
   Championships with 14 goals and four assists in
   eight games

2001   Joined Dynamo Moscow

Glossary

All-Star: one of a group of the best players, as voted by fans, who meet in a special game in the middle of the season

attacker: a skater who is on the ice to pass or score

checked: guarded closely by an opponent

contract: an agreement that a player and a team both sign. A contract states a player's salary and other details of the player's job with the team.

defender: a player whose job it is to stop the other team from scoring

division: in the NHL, one of three sets of teams in each conference. The Capitals are in the Southeast Division of the Eastern Conference.

draft: a yearly event in which professional teams take turns choosing new players from a selected group

economy: the financial condition of a state or a country

general manager: in sports, the person who makes decisions about players on a team, such as how much to pay each player

goalie: a player who stands in front of the goal and tries to stop the other team from scoring

overtime: in hockey, an extra five-minute period played when a game is tied after three periods

period: part of a hockey game. Hockey games have three periods.

Stanley Cup: the trophy awarded to the team that wins the NHL championship

wrist shot: a shot made by pulling your upper wrist back and snapping your lower wrist forward while sweeping the stick blade along the ice.

Further Reading & Websites

Kennedy, Mike, and Mark Stewart. *Score! The Action and Artistry of Hockey's Magnificent Moment*. Minneapolis: Millbrook Press, 2011.

McMahon, Dave. *Alex Ovechkin: NHL Superstar*. Edina, MN: ABDO Publishing Company, 2011.

Savage, Jeff. *Sidney Crosby*. Minneapolis: Lerner Publications Company, 2009.

The Official Site of the National Hockey League
http://www.nhl.com
The NHL's official website provides fans with the latest scores, schedules, and standings, as well as biographies and statistics of players.

Sports Illustrated Kids
http://www.sikids.com
The *Sports Illustrated Kids* website covers all sports, including hockey.

Washington Capitals: The Official Site
http://www.capitals.nhl.com
The official website of the Washington Capitals that includes the team's results and schedule, late-breaking news, biographies of Alex Ovechkin and other players, team history, and more.

Index

Photo Acknowledgments

The images in this book are used with the permission of: © Abelimages/Getty Images, p. 4; © Nick Turchiaro/Icon SMI, p. 5; © Graig Abel/NHLI via Getty Images, pp. 6, 7; © Bayda127/Dreamstime.com, p. 9; © IHA/Icon SMI, p. 10; © Oleg Nikishin/Getty Images, p. 13; © Jeff Vinnick/Getty Images, p. 14; AP Photo/Karl DeBlaker, p. 15; AP Photo/Chuck Stoody, CP, p. 17; © Al Bello/Getty Images, p. 18; © Bruce Bennett/Getty Images, pp. 19, 22, 26; © Geoff Burke/US Presswire, pp. 21, 24; AP Photo/Stephen J. Boitano, p. 23; © Jim McIsaac/Getty Images, p. 25; AP Photo/Susan Walsh, p. 27; © Gregg Forwerck/NHLI via Getty Images, p. 28; © G. Fiume/Getty Images, p. 29.

Front cover: © G. Fiume/Getty Images.

Main body text set in Caecilia LT std 55 Roman 16/28. Typeface provided by Linotype AG.